YOU ARE A SCIENTIST

Everything Science

Marcia S. Freeman

Rourke

Publishing LLC
Vero Beach, Florida 32964

PHOTO CREDITS: Cover, title page, pages 9, 10, 11, 13, 16, 17 © Lynn M. Stone; pages 4, 6, ©Flanagan Publishing pages 11, 15, 19 © Lois Nelson; pages 14, 18, 21 © Photodisc; page 20 © Armentrout

Library of Congress Cataloging-in-Publication

Freeman, Marcia S.
    You are a scientist (Everything science)

ISBN 1-59515-126-5

Printed in the USA

LK/BK

Table of Contents

Exploring Your World

You have been **exploring** your world since you were born.

As you feel the smooth pages of this book, see their colorful pictures, and hear the sound of pages turning, you are gathering information about your world.

Sometimes exploring is messy.

Gathering Information

Like you, scientists use their **senses** to gather information. So, you are a scientist when you look at, smell, feel, and listen to things.

You are noticing **attributes** such as color, texture, location, symmetry, age, shape, size, and smell.

What do you think these puppies feel like?

What do you think this flower smells like?

Asking Questions

Like you, scientists notice and wonder about things. They ask questions about them. What? Where? How? Why?

What plants can you find here?

Where do antelopes live?

How far can I
kick this football?

Why do
roosters crow?

Finding Answers

How do you find the answers to your questions? Like scientists, you study and you read.

This girl can find good information about her pet turtle in books.

Like scientists, you collect things you are studying to take a closer look.

What might this young scientist catch in his net?

Recording Information

You are a scientist when you observe living things first-hand. You may build a temporary **habitat** in a **terrarium** or a tank.

You may study an unusual pet.

Sharing Information

You are a scientist when you try something out, when you **experiment**.

What do you think would happen if one team let go of the rope?

What science question have *you* answered by trying something out?

Does a pulley make lifting easier?

Scientists **record** what they see and find in a notebook.

August 18
Today my dad took us all out on a boat. We went fishing. Christian caught a barracuda. It had sharp teeth!

A young scientist recorded information about a barracuda. What could you observe and write about the shells?

All scientists share what they learn
about their world.

Glossary

attributes (AH truh BYOOTZ) — features of something, such as color and texture

experiment (ek SPER uh munt) — a test to find something out

exploring (ek SPLOR ing) — investigating

habitat (HAB uh TAT) — area where animals or plants live

noticing (NOHT us ing) — seeing something

record (ree KORD) — put information in a book or on a tape

senses (SENS uz) — sight, hearing, touch, taste, and smell

terrarium (tuh RER ee um) — a plant habitat in a tank

Index

Science Standard: The Nature of Science
People can learn about things by observing carefully.
Describing things accurately is important in science.
Everyone can do science.

Marcia S. Freeman loves writing science books for children. A Cornell University graduate, she has taught science and writing to students from elementary to high school, and their teachers too! Her 50 books also include children's fiction and writing education texts for teachers.